Evaluate Habitat Use and Population Dynamics of Lampreys in Cedar Creek

BPA Contract #200001400

Annual Report

Prepared by:

Jennifer Stone
Timothy Sundlov
Scott Barndt
Travis Coley

U. S. Fish and Wildlife Service
Columbia River Fisheries Program Office
Habitat and Natural Production Team
9317 N. E. Highway 99, Suite I
Vancouver, Washington 98665 USA

March 31, 2001

Abstract

Pacific lamprey (*Lampetra tridentata*) in the Columbia River Basin have declined to a remnant of their pre-1940s populations and the status of the western brook lamprey (*L. richardsoni)* is unknown. Identifying the biological and ecological factors limiting lamprey populations is critical to their recovery, but little research has been conducted on these species within the Columbia River Basin. This ongoing, multi-year study examines lamprey populations in Cedar Creek, Washington, a third-order tributary to the Lewis River. Adult (n = 40), metamorphosed (n = 116), transforming (n = 10), and ammocoete (n = 870) stages from both species were examined in 2000. Lamprey were captured using adult fish ladders, rotary screw traps, and lamprey electrofishers, and spawning ground surveys were conducted. US Forest Service level II and strategic point-specific habitat surveys were conducted to assess habitat requirements of both adult and larval lamprey. Multivariate statistics will be applied to determine relationships between abundance and habitat.

Introduction

Three lamprey species (*Lampetra tridentata, L. ayresi,* and *L. richardsoni*) include the Columbia River Basin (CRB) within their geographic ranges (Kan 1975). Pacific lamprey (*L. tridentata*) in the CRB have declined to only a remnant of their pre-1940s populations (Close et al. 1995) and the status of *L. ayresi* and *L. richardsoni* is unknown. The ecological, economic, and cultural significance of these species is grossly underestimated (Kan 1975, Close et al. 1995). Though biological and ecological information for these species is available (e.g. Pletcher 1963, Beamish 1980, Richards 1980, Beamish and Levings 1991), few studies have been conducted within the CRB (Kan 1975, Hammond 1979). Actions are currently being considered for the recovery of Pacific lamprey populations in the CRB (Close et al. 1995).

Identifying biological and ecological factors that limit lamprey in the CRB is critical for their recovery. Availability and accessibility of suitable spawning habitat may limit the amount of reproduction that occurs within a basin. Factors influencing survival of early life history stages may be critical to determining recruitment to the population (Houde 1987). For example, Potter et al. (1986), and Young et al. (1990) suggest that larval lamprey (ammocoete) abundance is affected by water temperature and other physical habitat characteristics during early development.

The success of rehabilitating Pacific lamprey could depend on whether Pacific lamprey exhibit homing behavior. Their counterparts, the sea lamprey (*Petromyzon marinus*) do not home to natal streams (Bergstedt and Seelye 1995) but instead respond to a bile acid based larval pheromone released by conspecific larval lamprey (Bjerselius et al. 2000). If Pacific lamprey do exhibit homing behavior, it may be necessary to recognize ecologically significant units (ESU) in any rehabilitation effort, instead of focusing on the population as a whole.

This research represents the first year of a multi-year, baseline study to provide data on the population dynamics and habitat use of lamprey in Cedar Creek, a stream located within the CRB. The objectives of this research are to: 1. estimate the abundance of larval and adult lamprey and measure biological characteristics; 2. determine larval distribution and habitat use; 3. determine outmigrant timing of larvae and macropthalmia; 4. evaluate spawning habitat requirements; and 5. evaluate homing fidelity, survival rates, and ocean residence.

Life History

The Pacific lamprey (*Lamperta tridentata*) ranges from southern California to the Bearing Sea and Alaska and is both parasitic and anadromous. Adults enter the stream from July to October. Spawning takes place the following spring when water temperatures are 10 - 15 °C (Beamish 1980, Beamish and Levings 1991). Both sexes construct nests in gravel that are approximately 40 - 60 cm in diameter and less than 1 m in depth (Close et al. 1995). They deposit between 10,000 - 200,000 eggs and die within 3 - 36 days after spawning (Kan 1975, Pletcher 1963). Larvae hatch in about 19 days at 15 °C (Pletcher 1963) and spend 4 - 6 years as ammocoetes in fine sediment, pumping water through their branchial chamber, filtering diatoms, algae, and detritus (Beamish and Levings 1991). Pacific lamprey transform from ammocoetes to juveniles (macropthalmia) in July to October. The macropthalmia migrate to the ocean between late fall and spring (van de Wetering 1998). They spend 1 - 4 years as adults feeding as external parasites on marine fish (Beamish 1980).

The western brook lamprey (*Lamperta richardsoni*) ranges from southern California to British Columbia (Scott and Crossman 1973). It is non-parasitic and completes its life cycle in freshwater, obtaining lengths of 160 mm (Close et al. 1995). Spawning occurs from late April to early July when temperatures range from 7.8 - 20 °C. Nests are commonly constructed by males in gravel 16 - 100 mm and are 100 - 125 mm in diameter and 50 mm in depth (Scott and Crossman 1973). A nest may contain up to 30 spawning adults and can be occupied by several different groups over a 10 - 14 day period (Scott and Crossman 1973). Eggs hatch in 10 days at 10 - 15.5 °C. After hatching, blind larval (ammocoetes) move to areas of low flow and high organic matter. Larvae remain in the sediment nursery areas for 3-6 years, and feed similarly to Pacific lamprey ammocoetes. The mature ammocoetes metamorphose into adults from August to November and over-winter without feeding. Adults become sexually mature in March and die shortly after spawning.

Study Area

This study is being conducted in Cedar Creek, a third-order tributary to the Lewis River (Figure 1). The Lewis River enters the Columbia River at Columbia

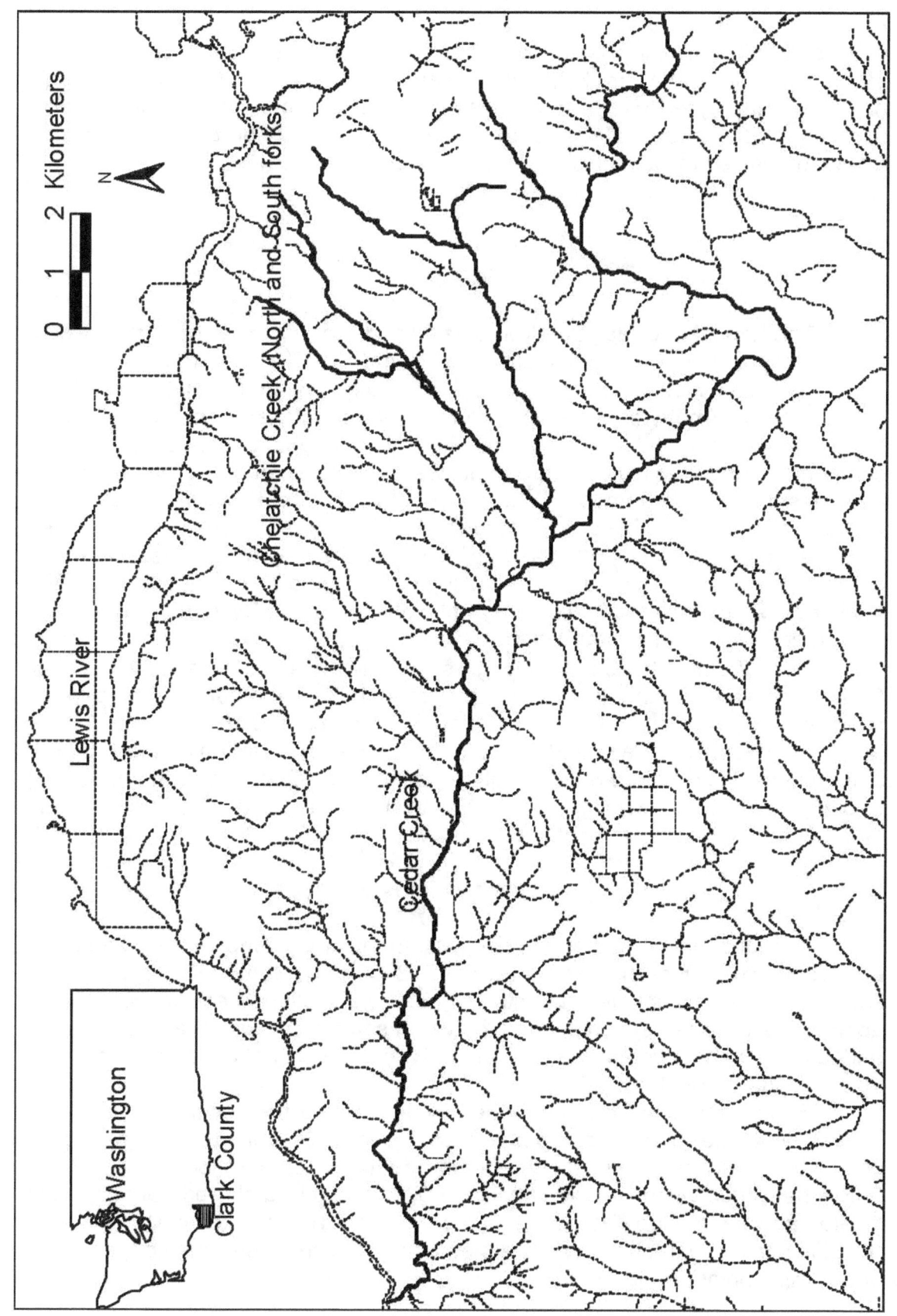

Figure 1. Cedar Creek in Clark County, Washington.

River mile 87. The Cedar Creek drainage includes 89.3 km^2 of diverse stream types and habitat conditions, contains five major tributaries (Chelatchie, Pup, Bitter, Rush, and John Creeks), and is inhabited by *L. tridentata*, *L richardsoni*, and possibly *L. ayresi* (D. Rawding, Washington Department of Fish and Wildlife, pers. comm). Access to Cedar Creek is uninhibited by either dams or by the effects of mainstem Columbia River hydropower development.

Methods

Habitat

The habitat of Cedar Creek was assessed from confluence of the Lewis River to approximately 2.5 km south of the Cedar Creek fork. A modified US Forest Service Level II survey was conducted to obtain approximate habitat characteristics (Anonymous 1997). Surveys were conducted from July 17, 2000 through August 15, 2000. The stream was divided into riffle and pool components and detailed measurements were recorded for every fifth to eighth component (depending upon the frequency) of each type. Refer to Table 1 for habitat characteristics that were recorded. Rosgen stream types (Rosgen 1996) were then assigned to each "measured" riffle and the stream was classified into reaches based on contiguous areas having similar stream types (Figure 2). All habitat data were entered into a Geographical Information System (GIS) for presentation and analysis purposes.

Hobo Tidbit® temperature loggers were deployed at three locations along Cedar Creek and another five were deployed in the four tributaries. Temperature data were collected every four hours throughout the course of the study.

Flow data were recorded by USGS at the Heisson station on the East Fork of the Lewis River (Figure 3). In addition, Washington State Department of Ecology deployed a flow gage at the Grist Mill bridge in Cedar Creek during fall of 2000, but these data are not yet available.

Lamprey Density

The longitudinal distribution of anadromous larval lamprey and western brook adults was assessed from August 15, 2000 to September 8, 2000 by sampling 18 60 m sections of the stream. Sample sections were spaced 1000 m apart. An additional section (located between sample sections 9 and 10) was added in an area having a Rosgen stream type that was not observed in the first 18 sections (Figure 4).

Each sample section was further divided into six transects that were spaced 10 m apart from one another. Each transect contained two sampling points; the sampling points on even-numbered transects were located at 1/3 and 2/3 of the wetted width and the sampling points on odd-numbered transects were located at water's edge (Figure 5). Sampling points had an area of 0.79 m^2. Specific habitat characteristics were measured at each sample section, transect, and sample point (Table 2).

Table 1. Habitat characteristics measured during habitat survey, Cedar Creek, Washington.

Unit Characteristic	All Units	Measured Riffles	Measured Pools
Length	X	X	X
Average Width	X	X	X
Maximum Depth	X	X	X
Average Depth	X	X	X
Depth at Pool Tail Crest	X		X
Percent Substrate (sand, gravel, cobble, bedrock, boulder)	X	X	X
Bank Stability	X	X	X
Large Woody Debris	X	X	X
Densiometer		X	X
Bankful Width		X	
Bankful Depth (at 1/4, 1/2, and 3/4 wetted width)		X	
Maximum Bankful Depth		X	
Flood Plain Depth		X	
Flood Plain Width		X	
Inside Riparian Vegetation Class		X	X
Outside Riparian Vegetation Class		X	X
Overstory Vegetation Class		X	X
Understory Vegetation Class		X	X
Temperature		X	X
Wolman Pebble Count		X*	

*also extended into downstream pool

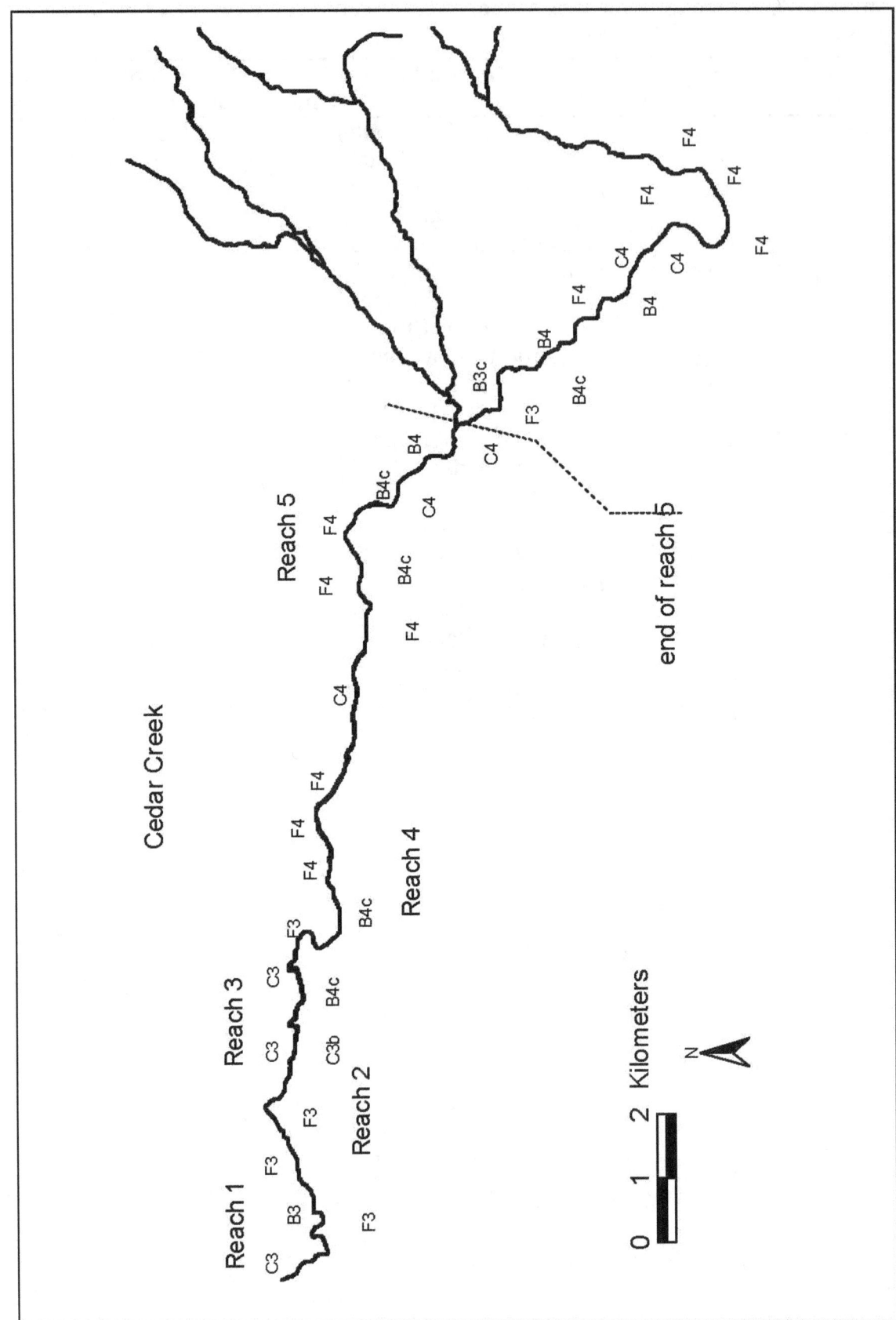

Figure 2. Rosgen stream type and reach designations.

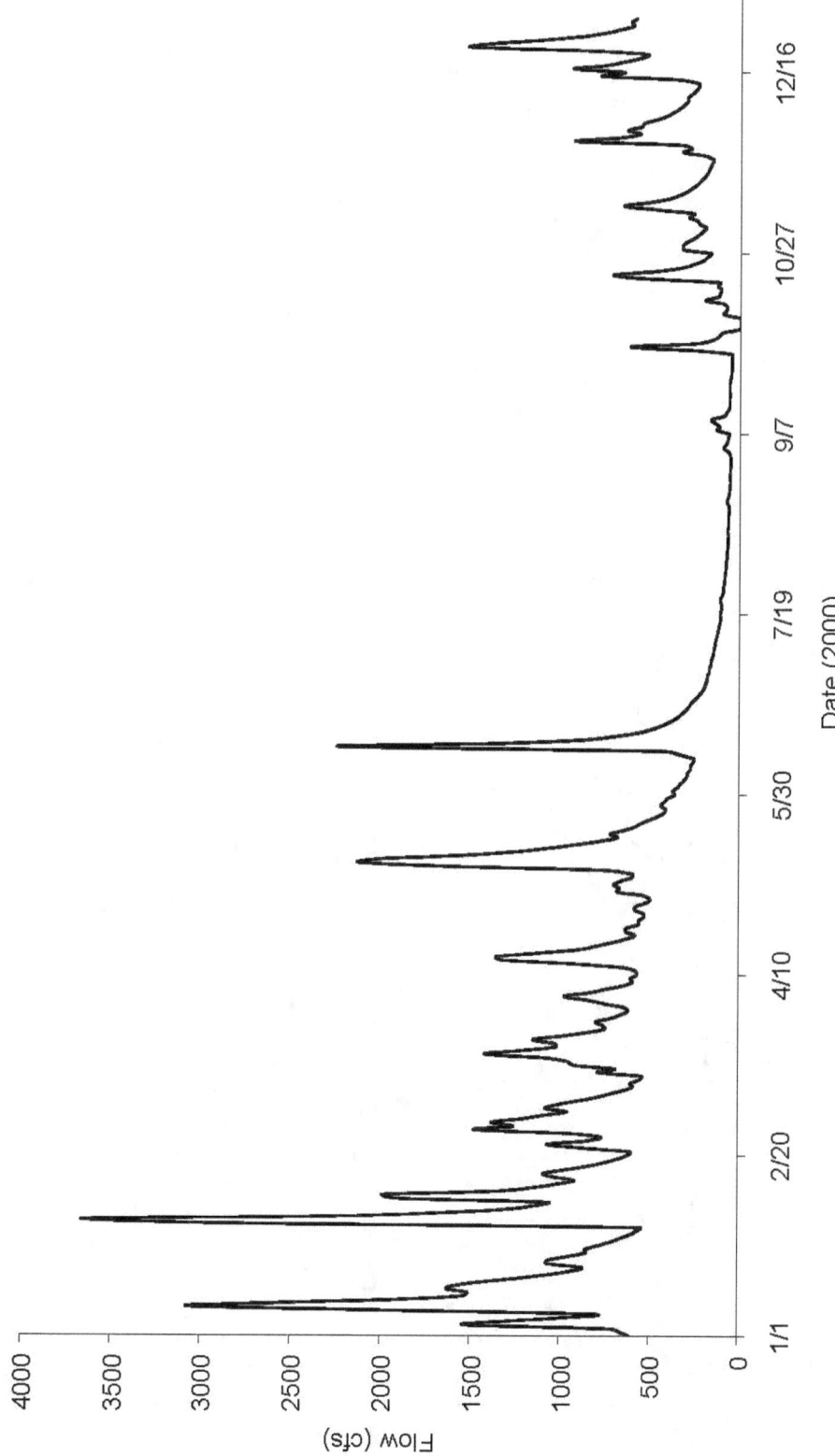

Figure 3. Flow data for the East Fork Lewis River collected by USGS at the Heisson Station, Washington.

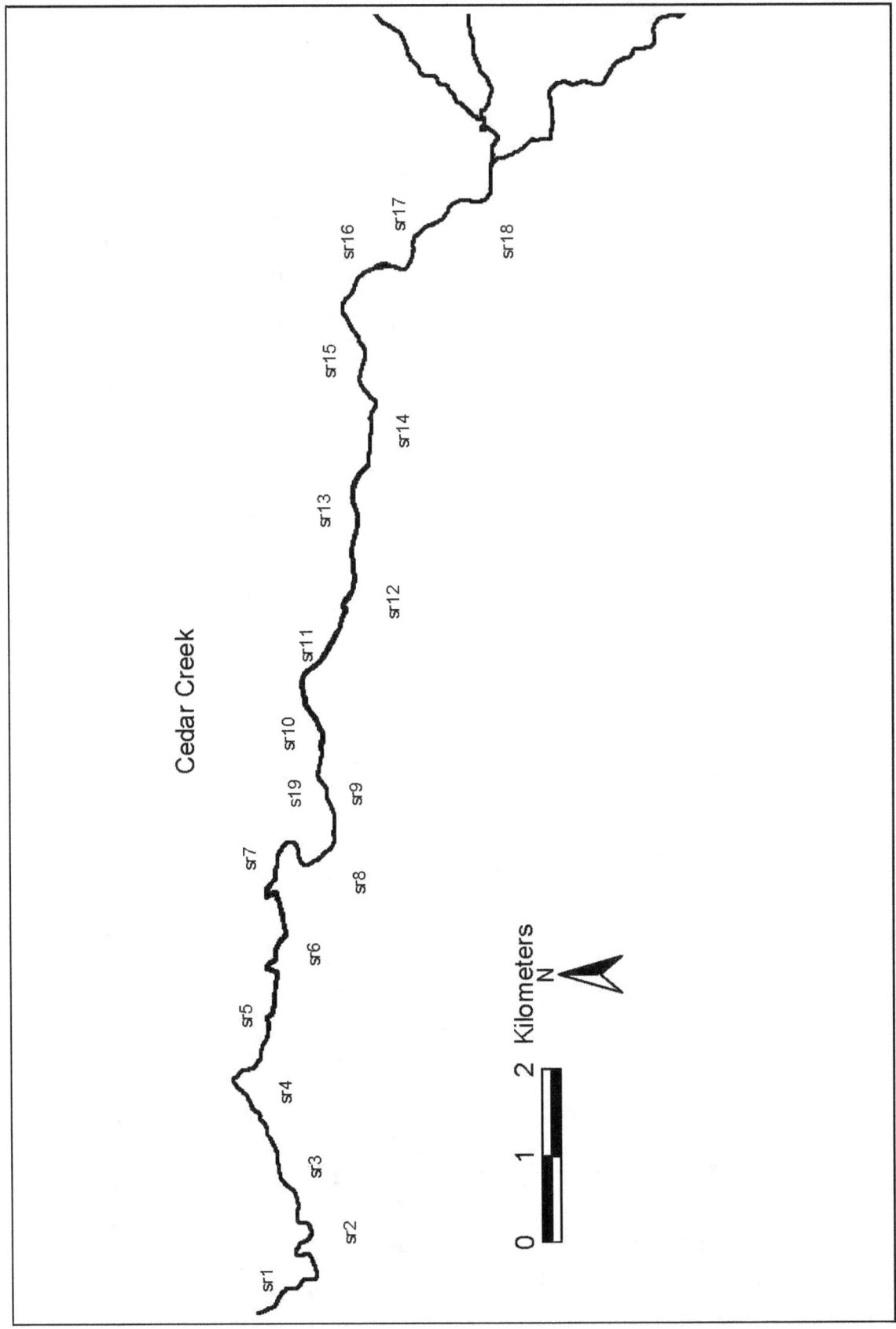

Figure 4. Sample reaches for electrofishing survey, Cedar Creek, Washington.

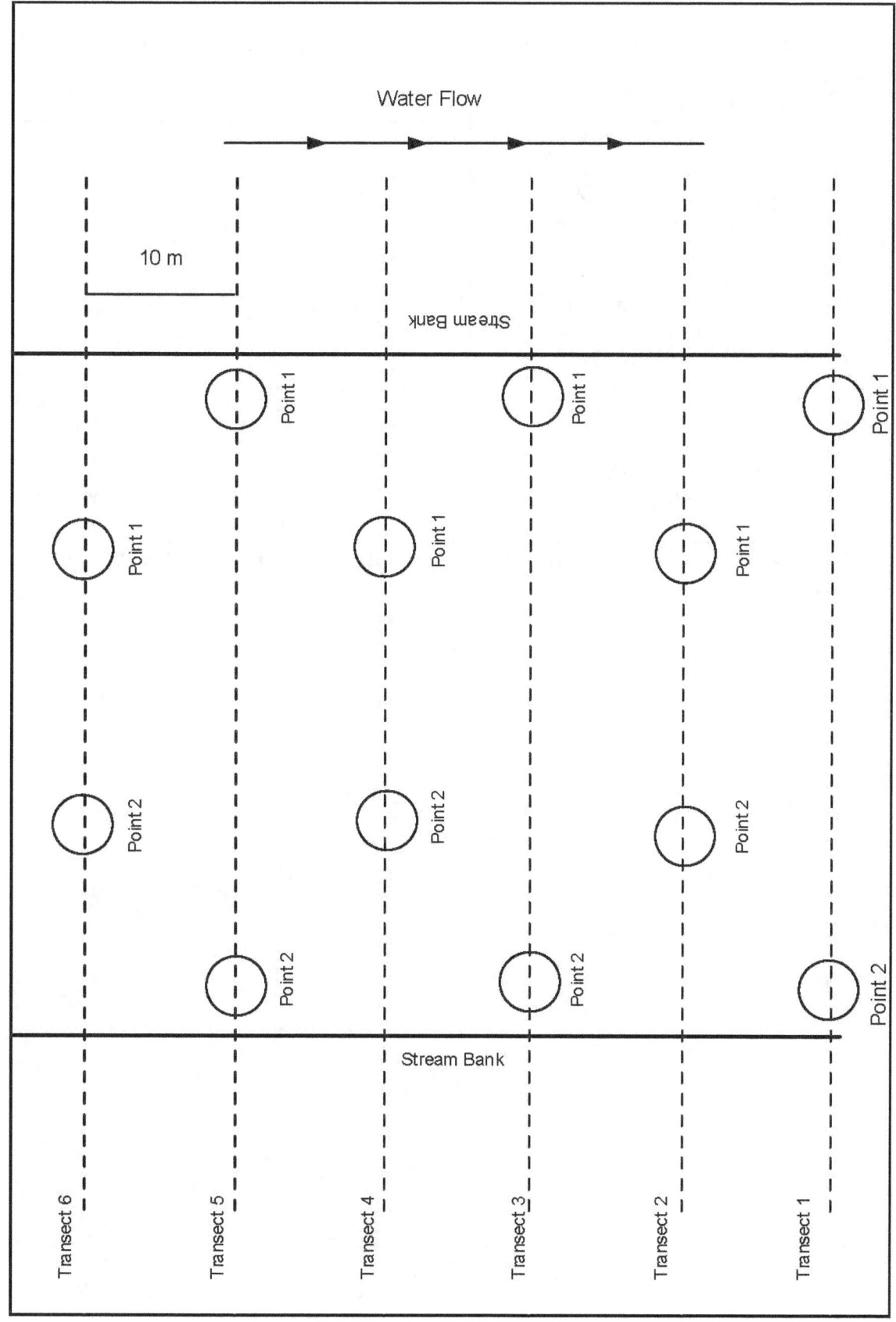

Figure 5. Transect and point layout for each sample reach during the electrofishing survey, Cedar Creek, Washington.

Table 2. Habitat characteristics measured at each sample point, Cedar Creek, Washington.

Habitat Characteristic	Sample Reach	Transect	Point
Water Temperature	X		
pH	X		
Dissolved Oxygen (%)	X		
Dissolved Oxygen (mg/L)	X		
Conductivity	X		
Specific Conductivity	X		
Gradient	X		
GPS Waypoint	X		
Wetted Width		X	
Densiometer		X	
Depth			X
Velocity			X
Percent Substrate*			X
Fine Substrate Depth			X
Bycatch			X

* organic debris, clay and silt, sand, small gravel, large gravel, cobble, boulder, and bedrock

Larval lamprey were captured from each sample point by 70% depletion electrofishing (Pajos and Weise 1994). Each point was sampled for 90 seconds per pass, with a minimum of two and a maximum of five passes. Lamprey measuring ≤30 mm could not be effectively depleted, therefore they were enumerated but not used in any analyses. Captured lamprey were anesthetized with MS-222 (Summerfeldt and Smith 1990), identified to species, and measured for length and weight. A sample of lamprey were euthanized and brought back to the lab for statolith analysis (n = 32) and genetic analyses (n = 53). Population estimates, standard errors, and probability of capture were calculated using the CAPTURE software (White 1978).

Outmigrants

Outmigrant lamprey were captured by a floating rotary screw trap (constructed by E. G. Solutions, Inc., Corvallis, OR) with a five-foot diameter cone placed in a pool upstream of Grist Mill falls in Cedar Creek. The trap operated from March 13, 2000 until December 31, 2000 and was checked daily during high flows and approximately every other day during low flow conditions. The cone was raised when the revolutions fell below 2 rpm or rose above 18 rpm, or in other adverse conditions. Lamprey were anesthetized, identified to species, and measured for length and weight. Trap efficiency and outmigrant abundance was estimated through mark/recapture (Thedinga et al. 1994). Ammocoetes were marked using colored elastomer injections and macrpthalmia and adults were marked with micro-jet injections, fin clips, and/or coded wire tags (CWT) (Bergstedt et al. 1993). Marked individuals were released upstream of the trap (ammocoetes approximately 50 m, and macrpthalmia approximately 2 km) and recaptured individuals were released approximately 50 m downstream of the trap.

Anadromous Adults

Adult anadromous lamprey were captured in the adult ladder at the Grist Mill falls. Initially, a box trap (Purvis 1985) also was deployed, but was removed because if its failure to trap adult lamprey. Lamprey were anesthetized, measured for length and weight, and marked with a passive integrated transponder (PIT) tag and a dorsal fin clip.

One snorkeling survey was conducted on June 22, 2000 below Grist Mills Falls in an attempt to capture and mark adult lamprey.

Spawning

Lamprey nests were identified by weekly foot surveys during the spawning period. The section of Cedar Creek between Amboy and Roselius Bridge was also observed during a float trip on April 20, 2000. When possible, physical characteristics of nests were measured, including: nest dimensions, depth in the water column, habitat type, substrate type, and the amount of cover or shading.

GPS waypoints were collected at each nest when possible. Nests were not capped because it was difficult to determine the exact time they were created.

Results

Habitat

The portion of Cedar Creek that was assessed was divided into five reaches that had similar stream types. Seven Rosgen stream types were identified throughout the stream, ranging from B3 to F4.

Temperatures at Cedar Creek ranged from 0.95 to 23.7 °C. The lowest temperatures were recorded at each location for approximately three days during the third week of November. Temperatures recorded from the three loggers located on Cedar Creek differed by a maximum of 7.87 °C, with the mean difference only 1 °C. The mean temperature during the electrofishing survey was 15 °C.

Lamprey Density

Only one lamprey species other than Pacific lamprey was identified during the electrofishing survey, and that was the western brook lamprey (*L. richardsoni*) (n=1). However, genetic samples collected during the survey have not been analyzed, so the level of field misidentification is uncertain at this point. Adult Pacific lamprey and macropthalmia were not captured during our sampling efforts.

Four hundred and three ammocoetes and 10 transforming lamprey were collected. Estimated population, probability of capture, standard error, and density were calculated for each sample point (Appendix 1). Thirty percent of the points sampled had at least one lamprey, and the mean number of lamprey in these points was six. The maximum number of lamprey > 30 mm captured at a single point was 28, and the density associated with this point was 35 lamprey/m^2.

Multivariate statistics will be used to associate lamprey density with habitat characteristics. Other statistical analyses will be used to associate lamprey density with position in the stream (water's edge vs 1/3 and 2/3).

Maximum, mean, and minimum lengths of ammocoetes were 128, 51.2, and 10 mm respectively. For transforming lamprey, maximum, mean, and minimum lengths were 113, 100, and 95 mm respectively. Weights were difficult to measure for smaller fish, but a regression was calculated on the length/weight data that were collected (Figure 6). The model for lamprey length and weight is: $y = 5E\text{-}06x^{2.7379}$. Sex was impossible to determine during field examinations. Statolith and genetic samples will be processed as soon as possible to determine the age structure.

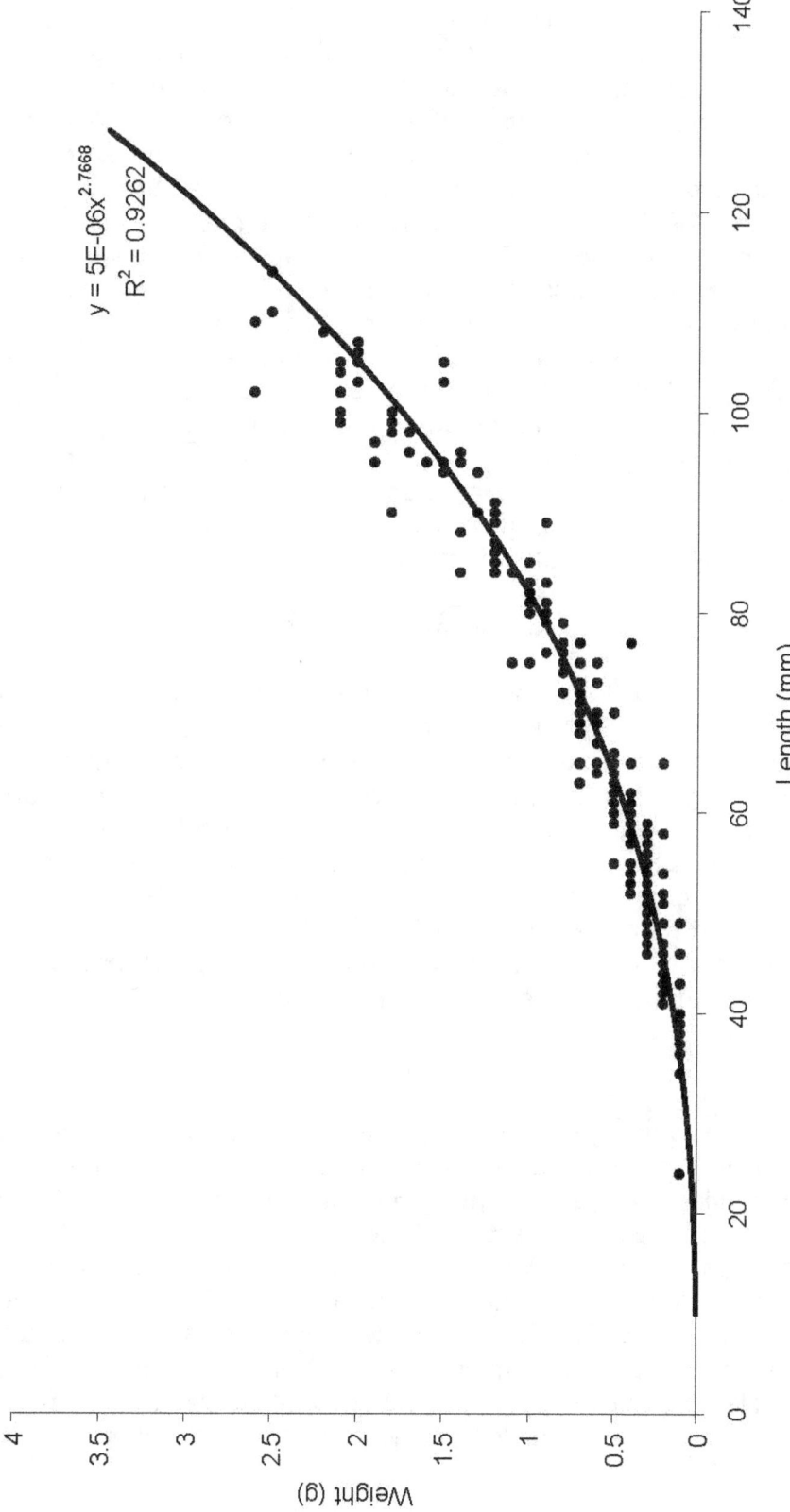

Figure 6. Regression of lamprey length to weight for fish captured during electrofishing survey, Cedar Creek, Washington.

13

Outmigrants

The floating rotary screw trap fished for approximately 276 days during sampling year 2000. Fourteen adult western brook lamprey were captured. Maximum, mean, and minimum western brook lamprey adult lengths were 145, 116, and 99 mm, respectively. Four hundred and sixty-seven ammocoetes and 116 macropthalmia were captured (Figure 7). Twenty ammocoetes and 10 macropthalmia were recaptured. Only two western brook lamprey ammocoetes were identified, all others were Pacific lamprey. However, genetic analyses will be conducted to verify the accuracy of field identifications.

Maximum, mean, and minimum lengths of ammocoetes were 143, 89.1, and 32 mm, respectively. Maximum, mean and minimum lengths of macropthalmia were 164, 124.8, and102 mm, respectively. The length to weight regression for ammocoetes was similar to the model reported above and the model for macropthalmia length and weight is : $y = 1E\text{-}05x^{2.587}$ with an $r^2 = 0.825$.

Most outmigrants moved during periods of increased flow, such as in spring melt periods and fall rain events (Figure 8). A few also moved during early summer, but the number of outmigrants decreased greatly during August, September, and October. Macropthalmia were in greatest numbers during November, whereas ammocoetes dominated the spring catch.

Anadromous Adults

Twenty-six Pacific lamprey were captured in the adult ladder. Adults were captured between April 16, 2000 and October 22, 2000. Maximum, mean, and minimum Pacific lamprey adult lengths were 610, 549, and 461 mm, respectively. Too few fish (n = 2) were recaptured to estimate spawning run abundance.

Three lamprey were observed on June 22, 2000 below the Grist Mill falls during a snorkeling survey. Only one was captured and tagged. These lamprey were observed "feeding" on a moribund spring chinook that had been tagged by Washington Department of Fish and Wildlife (WDFW).

Homing behavior cannot be assessed until the outmigrant lamprey marked with CWTs begin returning to Cedar Creek.

Spawning

Thirteen spawning ground surveys were conducted during the spawning period (April 6, 2000 through July 6, 2000). One hundred and thirty-two lamprey nests were identified and many of them were marked using GPS (Figure 9). Sixty-six were Pacific lamprey nests, forty-two were western brook lamprey, and the remaining were unknown. Pacific lamprey nest density was most abundant near the mouth of Cedar Creek and downstream of the Chelatchie forks.

Fifty percent of the Pacific lamprey nests were created in pool-tailouts, 33 percent were in riffles, and the remaining were in glides. Eighty-five percent of western brook lamprey nests were created in pool-tailouts, and seven percent were made in each riffles and glides. Mean area of Pacific lamprey and western

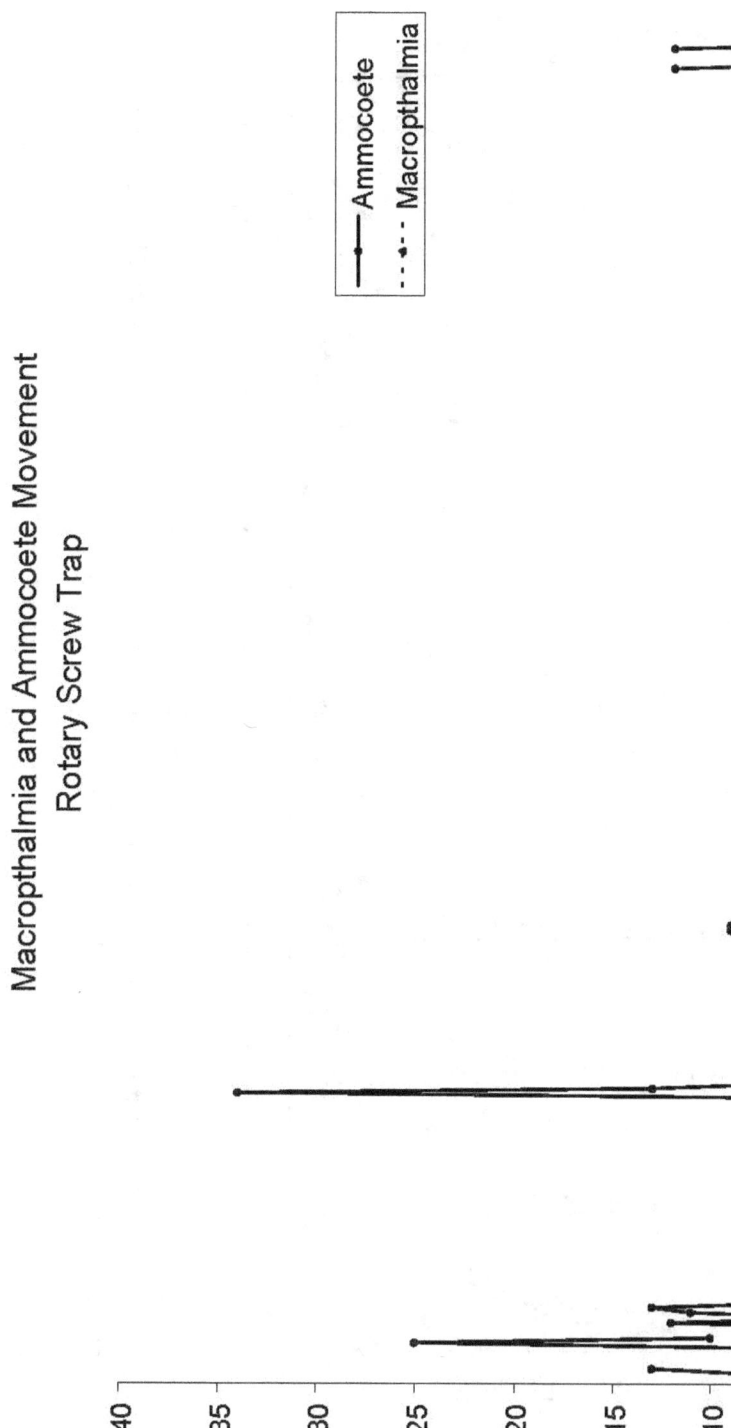

Macropthalmia and Ammocoete Movement
Rotary Screw Trap

Figure 7. Outmigrant movement in Cedar Creek, Washington. Fish captured by rotary screw trap positioned above the Grist Mill bridge.

15

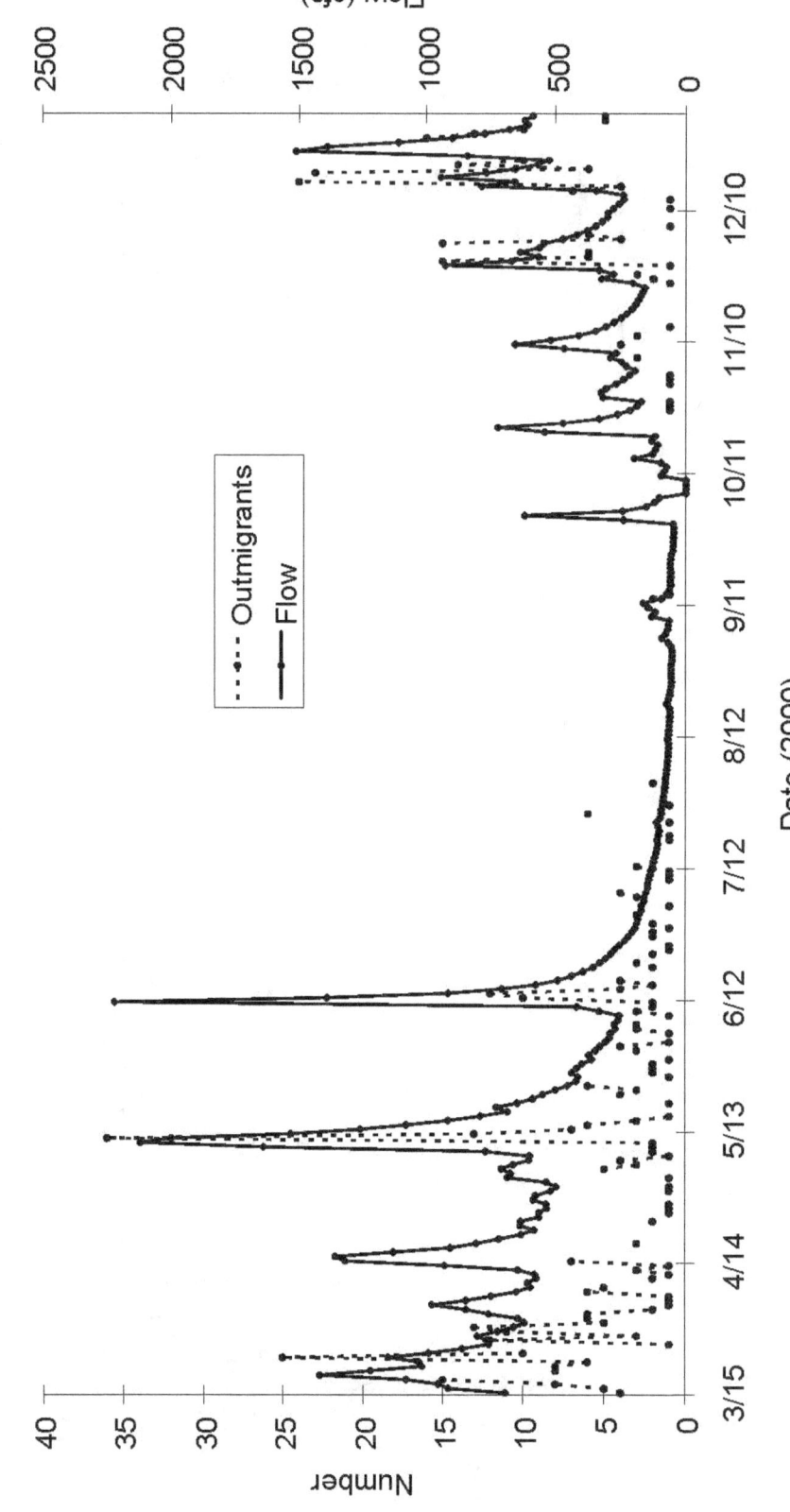

East Fork Lewis River Flow and Cedar Creek Outmigrant Abundance

Figure 8. Outmigrant movement in Cedar Creek, Washington. Flow data recorded by USGS in the East Fork Lewis River at the Heisson station.

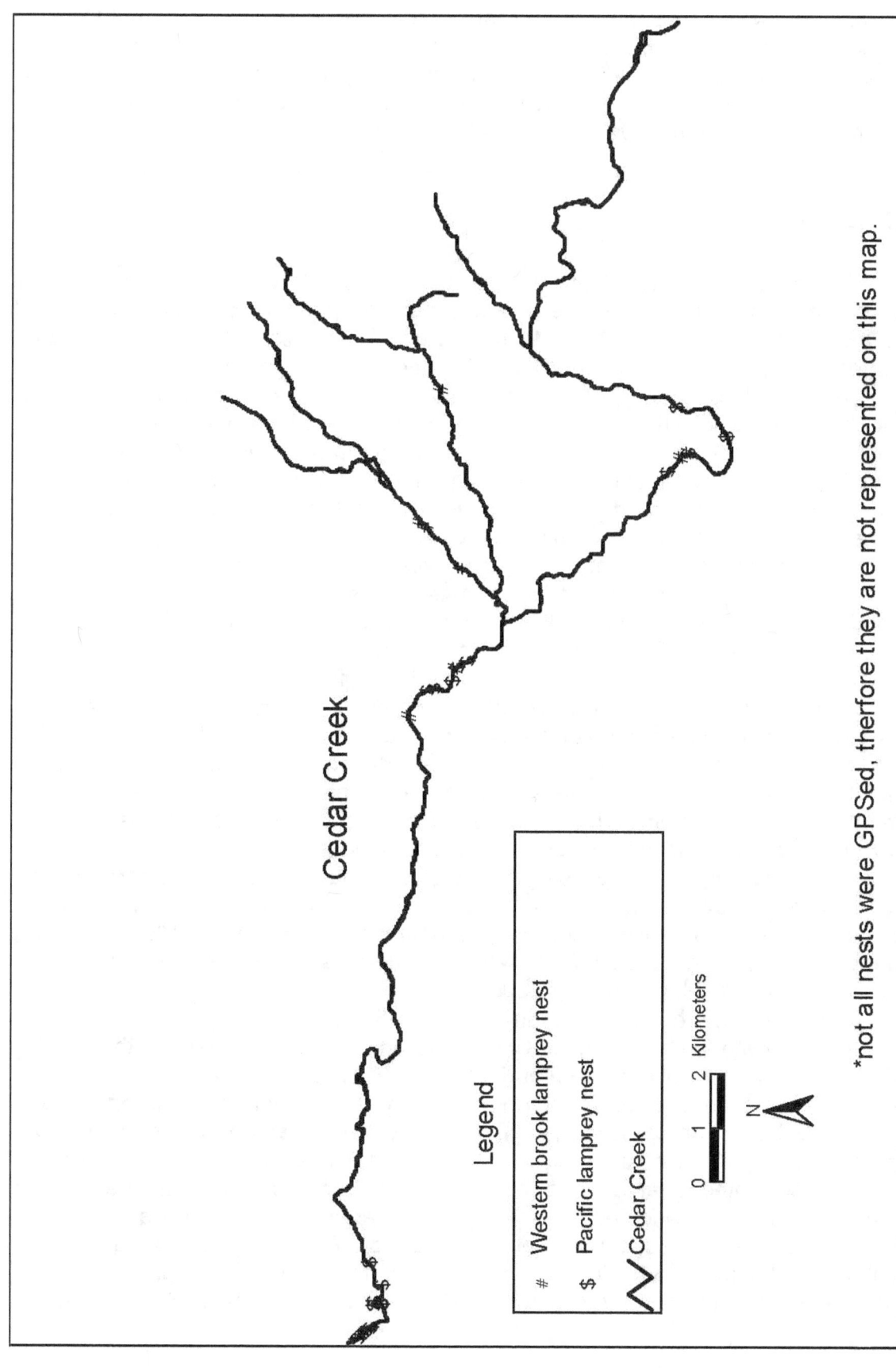

Figure 9. Lamprey nests observed in Cedar Creek, Washington, during the spawning ground surveys.

brook nests was 0.82 and 0.17 m², respectively. Mean depth of water at the Pacific lamprey and western brook nests was 0.4 and 0.29 m, respectively. Nests were often constructed in fine and gravel substrate, and rarely in cobble. It was empirically observed that Pacific lamprey tended to build nests in larger diameter substrate than western brook lamprey.

Discussion

Pacific and western book lamprey are active in Cedar Creek through much of the year. Adult Pacific lamprey enter the creek during June and September. It is uncertain whether June migrants immediately spawn or if they over winter as do the September migrants. Both species begin to move during the spawning period, which lasts from April to June. Larval lamprey are distributed throughout much of the creek, with greatest densities associated with areas containing low flow and fine sediments. Most Pacific lamprey metamorphose between August and September and peak movements of macropthalmia occur during high water events in the fall. Peak ammocoete movement occurs during the spring, but it is uncertain if this is active or passive movement.

There seems to be more Pacific lamprey than western brook lamprey, but this may be a result of incorrect field identifications. Studies are currently being conducted with USGS Biological Research Division at Cook, Washington to quantify the level of misidentification. This trend also may be a result of sample location, migratory behavior, and spawning distribution.

The adult traps at Cedar Creek are not efficient in catching adult lamprey. Unfortunately a small portion of the Cedar Creek flow is directed through the adult ladder, therefore lamprey most likely are drawn to the falls. The box trap did not catch adult lamprey in Cedar Creek though it has successfully captured adult lamprey in other systems (Purvis 1985). Its ineffectiveness may be related to its physical location, and in 2001 it will be repositioned.

Pacific lamprey are passing over the falls and spawning upstream. Based on nests and spawning adults observed in 2000 from the 1999 spawning run, Pacific lamprey made use of spawning habitat located above the falls. Spawning ground surveys conducted in 2001 will verify the extent of Pacific lamprey passage at Grist Mill falls during 2000.

Pacific lamprey spawned throughout Cedar Creek and western brook lamprey spawned in both forks of Chelatchie and on Cedar Creek North of the Chelatchie forks. Spawning habitat did not appear to be a limiting factor.

Distribution and density of larval lamprey is likely dependent upon point-specific habitat characteristics. A logistic will be performed on the electrofishing data collected from Cedar Creek to determine which habitat variables were most closely associated to larval. Potter et al. (1986) observed that ammocoete density was directly affected by environmental variables such as organic material, shade, eddies, current velocity, substrate particle size, and depth of substrate. Malmqvist (1980) observed that larval lamprey select burrowing habitat according to current velocity, water depth, and substrate. Beamish and

Lowartz (1996) related larval density to the percentage of medium-fine sand and organic matter in the substrate.

Population estimates per point were associated with high standard error due to low numbers of lamprey captured. Population estimates of larval lamprey across Cedar Creek have not been estimated. Presence and density of lamprey is extremely site-specific, and the general habitat surveys conducted in this study were too vague for a precise estimate of abundance. Pajos and Weise (1994) estimated larval populations through depletion sampling at randomly chosen transects. However their estimates were verified through lampricide treatments and a correction factor was added. They suggest that population estimates based solely upon depletion density data are inaccurate.

Outmigrant movement was closely associated with increased flow events. Unfortunately, sampling high water events is often difficult because of increased amounts of debris and safety issues. In these situations the trap either becomes inefficient or needs to be pulled. In the future, efforts will be made to fish freshets on a 24 hour basis, as these times may be critical movement periods.

Sampling efforts on Cedar Creek will continue for 2001 and an annual report, similar to this, will be delivered during the first months of 2002.

References

Anonymous. 1997. Stream inventory handbook level I and II. Forest Service, Pacific Northwest Region. 82 pp.

Beamish, R. J. 1980. Adult biology of the river lamprey (*Lampetra ayresi*) and the Pacific lamprey (*Lampetra tridentata*) from the Pacific coast of Canada. Canadian Journal of Fisheries and Aquatic Sciences. 37: 1906-1923.

Beamish, F. W. H., and S. Lowartz. 1996. Larval habitat of American brook lamprey. Canadian Journal of Fisheries and Aquatic Sciences. 53:693-700.

Beamish, R.J. and C. D. Levings. 1991. Abundance and freshwater migrations of the anadromous parasitic lamprey, *Lampetra tridentata* , in a tributary of the Fraser River, British Columbia. Canadian Journal of Fisheries & Aquatic Sciences 48:1250-1263.

Bergstedt, R. A., W. D. Swink, and J. G. Seelye. 1993. Evaluation of two locations for coded wire tags in larval and small parasitic-phase sea lampreys. North American Journal of Fisheries Management 13:609-612.

Bergstedt, R. A., and J. G. Seelye. 1995. Evidence for lack of homing by sea lampreys. Transactions of the American Fisheries Society 124:235-239.

Bjerselius R., L. Weiming, J. H. Teeter, J. G. Seelye, P. B. Johnsen, P. J. Maniak, G. C. Grant, C. N. Polkinghorne, and P. W. Sorensen. 2000. Direct behavioral evidence that unique bile acids released by larval sea Lamprey (*Petromyzon marinus*) function as a migratory pheromone. Canadian Journal of Fisheries and Aquatic Sciences 57:557-569.

Close, D. A., M. Fitzpatrick, H. Li, B. Parker, D. Hatch, and G. James. 1995. Status report of the Pacific lamprey (Lampetra tridentata) in the Columbia River Basin. Report (Contract 95BI39067) to Bonneville Power Administration, Portland, Oregon.

Hammond, R. J. 1979. Larval biology of the Pacific lamprey, *Entosphenus tridentatus* (Gairdner), of the Potlach River, Idaho. MS thesis. University of Idaho, Moscow.

Houde, E. D. 1987. Fish early life history dynamics and recruitment variability. American Fisheries Society Symposium 2 pp. 17-29.

Kan, T. T. 1975. Systematics, variation, distribution, and biology of lampreys of the genus *Lampetra* in Oregon. PhD dissertation. Oregon State University, Corvalis, OR. 194 pp.

Malmqvist, B. 1980. Habitat selection of larval brook lampreys (*Lampetra planeri*, Bloch) in a South Swedish stream. Oecologia 45:35-38.

Pajos, T. A. and J. G. Weise. 1994. Estimating populations of larval sea lamprey with electrofishing methods. North American Journal of Fisheries Management 14:580-587.

Pletcher, F. T. 1963. The life history and distribution of lampreys in the Salmon and certain other rivers in British Columbia, Canada. MS thesis, University of British Columbia, Vancouver, B. C. 195 pp.

Potter, I. C., R. W. Hilliard, J. S. Bradley, and R. J. McKay. 1986. The influence of environmental variables on the density of larval lampreys in different seasons. Oecologia 70:433-440.

Purvis, H.A., C.L. Chudy, E.L. King, Jr., and V.K. Dawson. 1985. Response of spawning-phase sea lampreys (Petromyzon marinus) to a lighted trap. Great Lakes Fishery Commission Technical Report Series number 42:15-25.

Richards, J. E. 1980. The freshwater life history of the anadromous Pacific lamprey, *Lampetra tridentata*. MS thesis, University of Guelph, Guelph, Ontario. 99 pp.

Rosgen, D and H. L. Silvey. 1994. Applied River Morphology. Wildland Hydrology, Pagosa Springs, Colorado.

Scott, W. B. and E. J. Crossman. 1973. Freshwater Fishes of Canada. Canadian Government Publishing Centre, Ottawa, Canada. 966 pp.

Summerfeldt, R.C. and L.S. Smith. 1990. Anethesia, surgery, and related techniques. Pages 213-272 in C.B. Schreck and P.B. Moyle, editors. Methods for fish biology. American Fisheries Society, Bethesda, Maryland.

Thedinga, J. F., M. L. Murphy, S. W. Johnson, J. M. Lorenz, and K. V. Koski. 1994. Determination of salmonid smolt yield with rotary-screw traps In the Situk River, Alaska, to predict effects of glacial flooding. North American Journal of Fisheries Management 14:837-851.

White, G. C., K. P. Burnham, D. L. Otis, and D. R. Anderson. 1978. User's Manual for Program CAPTURE. Utah State University Press, Logan, Utah. 40 pp.

Young, R. J., J. R. M. Kelso, and J. G. Weise. 1990. Occurrence, relative abundance, and size of landlocked sea lamprey (*Petromyzon marinus*) ammocoetes in relation to stream characteristics in the Great Lakes. Canadian Journal of Fisheries and Aquatic Sciences 47:1173-1178.

van de Wetering, S. J. 1998. Aspects of life history characteristics and physiological processes in smolting Pacific lamprey, *Lamperta tridentata*, in a central Oregon stream. MS thesis, Oregon State University.

Vladykov, V.D. and W. I. Follett. 1965. *Lampetra richardsoni*, a new nonparasitic species of lamprey (Petromyzonidae) from western North America. Journal of Fisheries Research Board of Canada 22:139-158.

Appendix 1. Statistics from Capture Program for electrofishing survey, Cedar Creek.

ID Number	Population Estimate	SE	Probability of Capture	Density	ID Number	Population Estimate	SE	Probability of Capture	Density
SR1T1P1	6	0.94	0.43	7.59	SR5T1P2	1	0.00	0.99	1.27
SR1T1P2	0	0.00	0.00	0.00	SR5T2P1	0	0.00	0.00	0.00
SR1T2P1	0	0.00	0.00	0.00	SR5T2P2	0	0.00	0.00	0.00
SR1T2P2	0	0.00	0.00	0.00	SR5T3P1	0	0.00	0.00	0.00
SR1T3P1	0	0.00	0.00	0.00	SR5T3P2	0	0.00	0.00	0.00
SR1T3P2	0	0.00	0.00	0.00	SR5T4P1	0	0.00	0.00	0.00
SR1T4P1	0	0.00	0.00	0.00	SR5T4P2	0	0.00	0.00	0.00
SR1T4P2	0	0.00	0.00	0.00	SR5T5P1	0	0.00	0.00	0.00
SR1T5P1	0	0.00	0.00	0.00	SR5T5P2	15	0.92	0.83	18.99
SR1T5P2	0	0.00	0.00	0.00	SR5T6P1	0	0.00	0.00	0.00
SR1T6P1	0	0.00	0.00	0.00	SR5T6P2	0	0.00	0.00	0.00
SR1T6P2	0	0.00	0.00	0.00	SR6T1P1	2	0.00	0.99	2.53
SR2T1P1	11	0.95	0.55	13.92	SR6T1P2	0	0.00	0.00	0.00
SR2T1P2	0	0.00	0.00	0.00	SR6T2P1	0	0.00	0.00	0.00
SR2T2P1	1	0.00	0.99	1.27	SR6T2P2	0	0.00	0.00	0.00
SR2T2P2	0	0.00	0.00	0.00	SR6T3P1	4	0.21	0.80	5.06
SR2T3P1	0	0.00	0.00	0.00	SR6T3P2	2	0.00	0.99	2.53
SR2T3P2	0	0.00	0.00	0.00	SR6T4P1	1	0.00	0.99	1.27
SR2T4P1	0	0.00	0.00	0.00	SR6T4P2	28	0.62	0.90	35.44
SR2T4P2	0	0.00	0.00	0.00	SR6T5P1	0	0.00	0.00	0.00
SR2T5P1	0	0.00	0.00	0.00	SR6T5P2	0	0.00	0.00	0.00
SR2T5P2	0	0.00	0.00	0.00	SR6T6P1	0	0.00	0.00	0.00
SR2T6P1	0	0.00	0.00	0.00	SR6T6P2	0	0.00	0.00	0.00
SR2T6P2	0	0.00	0.00	0.00	SR7T1P1	0	0.00	0.00	0.00
SR3T1P1	0	0.00	0.00	0.00	SR7T1P2	0	0.00	0.00	0.00
SR3T1P2	0	0.00	0.00	0.00	SR7T2P1	0	0.00	0.00	0.00
SR3T2P1	0	0.00	0.00	0.00	SR7T2P2	0	0.00	0.00	0.00
SR3T2P2	0	0.00	0.00	0.00	SR7T3P1	0	0.00	0.00	0.00
SR3T3P1	0	0.00	0.00	0.00	SR7T3P2	0	0.00	0.00	0.00
SR3T3P2	0	0.00	0.00	0.00	SR7T4P1	0	0.00	0.00	0.00
SR3T4P1	0	0.00	0.00	0.00	SR7T4P2	0	0.00	0.00	0.00
SR3T4P2	1	0.00	0.00	1.27	SR7T5P1	11	0.33	0.92	13.92
SR3T5P1	0	0.00	0.00	0.00	SR7T5P2	0	0.00	0.00	0.00
SR3T5P2	0	0.00	0.00	0.00	SR7T6P1	0	0.00	0.00	0.00
SR3T6P1	0	0.00	0.00	0.00	SR7T6P2	6	0.00	1.00	7.59
SR3T6P2	0	0.00	0.00	0.00	SR8T1P1	0	0.00	0.00	0.00
SR4T1P1	13	1.15	0.53	16.46	SR8T1P2	5	0.88	0.50	6.33
SR4T1P2	0	0.00	0.00	0.00	SR8T2P1				
SR4T2P1	0	0.00	0.00	0.00	SR8T2P2	0	0.00	0.00	0.00
SR4T2P2	0	0.00	0.00	0.00	SR8T3P1				
SR4T3P1	0	0.00	0.00	0.00	SR8T3P2	10	0.55	0.62	12.66
SR4T3P2	0	0.00	0.00	0.00	SR8T4P1	5	1.72	0.33	6.33
SR4T4P1	0	0.00	0.00	0.00	SR8T4P2	1	0.00	0.99	1.27
SR4T4P2	0	0.00	0.00	0.00	SR8T5P1	0	0.00	0.00	0.00
SR4T5P1	0	0.00	0.00	0.00	SR8T5P2	0	0.00	0.00	0.00
SR4T5P2	0	0.00	0.00	0.00	SR8T6P1	0	0.00	0.00	0.00
SR4T6P1	0	0.00	0.00	0.00	SR8T6P2	0	0.00	0.00	0.00
SR4T6P2	0	0.00	0.00	0.00	SR9T1P1	0	0.00	0.00	0.00
SR5T1P1	0	0.00	0.00	0.00	SR9T1P2	0	0.00	0.00	0.00

ID Number	Population Estimate	SE	Probability of Capture	Density	ID Number	Population Estimate	SE	Probability of Capture	Density
SR9T2P1	0	0.00	0.00	0.00	SR13T2P2	0	0.00	0.00	0.00
SR9T2P2	0	0.00	0.00	0.00	SR13T3P1	0	0.00	0.00	0.00
SR9T3P1	0	0.00	0.00	0.00	SR13T3P2	8	0.40	0.89	10.13
SR9T3P2	0	0.00	0.00	0.00	SR13T4P1	1	0.00	0.99	1.27
SR9T4P1	1	0.00	0.99	1.27	SR13T4P2	0	0.00	0.00	0.00
SR9T4P2	0	0.00	0.00	0.00	SR13T5P1	1	0.00	0.99	1.27
SR9T5P1	1	0.00	0.99	1.27	SR13T5P2	0	0.00	0.00	0.00
SR9T5P2	7	0.43	0.87	8.86	SR13T6P1	0	0.00	0.00	0.00
SR9T6P1	0	0.00	0.00	0.00	SR13T6P2	0	0.00	0.00	0.00
SR9T6P2	0	0.00	0.00	0.00	SR14T1P1	3	0.71	0.60	3.80
SR10T1P1	0	0.00	0.00	0.00	SR14T1P2	6	0.47	0.86	7.59
SR10T1P2	0	0.00	0.00	0.00	SR14T2P1	0	0.00	0.00	0.00
SR10T2P1	0	0.00	0.00	0.00	SR14T2P2	0	0.00	0.00	0.00
SR10T2P2	0	0.00	0.00	0.00	SR14T3P1	4	0.00	0.99	5.06
SR10T3P1	0	0.00	0.00	0.00	SR14T3P2	0	0.00	0.00	0.00
SR10T3P2	0	0.00	0.00	0.00	SR14T4P1	0	0.00	0.00	0.00
SR10T4P1					SR14T4P2	0	0.00	0.00	0.00
SR10T4P2	0	0.00	0.00	0.00	SR14T5P1	0	0.00	0.00	0.00
SR10T5P1	0	0.00	0.00	0.00	SR14T5P2	0	0.00	0.00	0.00
SR10T5P2	0	0.00	0.00	0.00	SR14T6P1	0	0.00	0.00	0.00
SR10T6P1	0	0.00	0.00	0.00	SR14T6P2	0	0.00	0.00	0.00
SR10T6P2	1	0.00	0.99	1.27	SR15T1P1	0	0.00	0.00	0.00
SR11T1P1	12	0.67	0.86	15.19	SR15T1P2	0	0.00	0.00	0.00
SR11T1P2	9	0.80	0.82	11.39	SR15T2P1	0	0.00	0.00	0.00
SR11T2P1	0	0.00	0.00	0.00	SR15T2P2	0	0.00	0.00	0.00
SR11T2P2	0	0.00	0.00	0.00	SR15T3P1	3	0.27	0.75	3.80
SR11T3P1	7	1.68	0.36	8.86	SR15T3P2	0	0.00	0.00	0.00
SR11T3P2	4	0.00	0.99	5.06	SR15T4P1	0	0.00	0.00	0.00
SR11T4P1	0	0.00	0.00	0.00	SR15T4P2	0	0.00	0.00	0.00
SR11T4P2	0	0.00	0.00	0.00	SR15T5P1	0	0.00	0.00	0.00
SR11T5P1	2	0.38	0.67	2.53	SR15T5P2	1	0.00	0.99	1.27
SR11T5P2	3	0.27	0.75	3.80	SR15T6P1	0	0.00	0.00	0.00
SR11T6P1	1	0.00	0.99	1.27	SR15T6P2	0	0.00	0.00	0.00
SR11T6P2	0	0.00	0.00	0.00	SR16T1P1	0	0.00	0.00	0.00
SR12T1P1	26	1.22	0.69	32.91	SR16T1P2	0	0.00	0.00	0.00
SR12T1P2	3	0.00	1.00	3.80	SR16T2P1	0	0.00	0.00	0.00
SR12T2P1	1	0.00	0.99	1.27	SR16T2P2	0	0.00	0.00	0.00
SR12T2P2	4	0.00	0.99	5.06	SR16T3P1	1	0.00	0.99	1.27
SR12T3P1	4	0.21	0.80	5.06	SR16T3P2	0	0.00	0.00	0.00
SR12T3P2	0	0.00	0.00	0.00	SR16T4P1	0	0.00	0.00	0.00
SR12T4P1	0	0.00	0.00	0.00	SR16T4P2	1	0.00	0.99	1.27
SR12T4P2	0	0.00	0.00	0.00	SR16T5P1	0	0.00	0.00	0.00
SR12T5P1	0	0.00	0.00	0.00	SR16T5P2	0	0.00	0.00	0.00
SR12T5P2	0	0.00	0.00	0.00	SR16T6P1	0	0.00	0.00	0.00
SR12T6P1	0	0.00	0.00	0.00	SR16T6P2	0	0.00	0.00	0.00
SR12T6P2	0	0.00	0.00	0.00	SR17T1P1	4	0.00	0.99	5.06
SR13T1P1					SR17T1P2				
SR13T1P2	0	0.00	0.00	0.00	SR17T2P1	0	0.00	0.00	0.00
SR13T2P1	0	0.00	0.00	0.00	SR17T2P2	0	0.00	0.00	0.00

Appendix 1. Continued

ID Number	Population Estimate	SE	Probability of Capture	Density
SR17T3P1	1	0.00	1.00	1.27
SR17T3P2	0	0.00	0.00	0.00
SR17T4P1	0	0.00	0.00	0.00
SR17T4P2	0	0.00	0.00	0.00
SR17T5P1	2	0.00	0.99	2.53
SR17T5P2	0	0.00	0.00	0.00
SR17T6P1	0	0.00	0.00	0.00
SR17T6P2	0	0.00	0.00	0.00
SR18T1P1	0	0.00	0.00	0.00
SR18T1P2	5	0.39	0.62	6.33
SR18T2P1	0	0.00	0.00	0.00
SR18T2P2	0	0.00	0.00	0.00
SR18T3P1				
SR18T3P2	0	0.00	0.00	0.00
SR18T4P1	0	0.00	0.00	0.00
SR18T4P2	5	0.00	0.99	6.33
SR18T5P1	10	0.00	0.99	12.66
SR18T5P2	12	0.67	0.86	15.19
SR18T6P1	0	0.00	0.00	0.00
SR18T6P2	0	0.00	0.00	0.00
SR19T1P1	2	0.00	0.99	2.53
SR19T1P2	0	0.00	0.00	0.00
SR19T2P1	2	0.00	0.99	2.53
SR19T2P2	1	0.00	0.99	1.27
SR19T3P1	18	0.98	0.69	22.78
SR19T3P2	0	0.00	0.00	0.00
SR19T4P1	0	0.00	0.00	0.00
SR19T4P2	0	0.00	0.00	0.00
SR19T5P1	0	0.00	0.00	0.00
SR19T5P2	0	0.00	0.00	0.00
SR19T6P1	0	0.00	0.00	0.00
SR19T6P2	0	0.00	0.00	0.00